# Fish Lu

Written by Emma Anthonisz

Illustrated by Parwinder Singh

Faith is with Mum and Dad.
They dash to get the train.

# Mum checks the bucket.

This will be such a fun trip!

bait

Faith runs up the dock.
Mum sets up the long rods.

ship

Faith flings her rod.

The fish will go in this chest.

Splash!

# Dad sits on the bench with a thump.

Faith swings her legs from the dock.
She sings as she waits.

Then it rains and Mum drops the bucket.

But the bait shop was shut!
Then Dad spots a big fish.

They had a fish and chip lunch!

# Talk about the story

Ask your child these questions:

**1** How did Faith and her family get to the sea?

**2** Who set up the fishing rods?

**3** Why did Mum have to go to the bait shop?

**4** Why did Dad get fish and chips for lunch?

**5** Have you ever been fishing? Would you like to go?

**6** How many different types of sea creatures can you think of?

Can your child retell the story in their own words?